The Military History of World War II
Volume 18

STRATEGIC DIRECTION OF WORLD WAR II

The Military History of World War II: Volume 18

STRATEGIC DIRECTION

OF WORLD WAR II

by Trevor Nevitt Dupuy

COL., U.S. ARMY, RET.

Franklin Watts, Inc.
575 Lexington Avenue, New York, N.Y. 10022

To Julia Crick,
who has helped me so greatly in this work

Library of Congress Catalog Card Number: 62-7382
Copyright © 1965 by Franklin Watts, Inc.
Printed in the United States of America

Contents

Strategic Direction of the War

Allied Organization and Coordination

BEFORE the United States entered World War II, there had been no regularly organized coordination of the Allied war effort. In the early days of the war there had been staff conferences between senior representatives of the French and British staffs; also there were French liaison officers permanently stationed with the British staffs in London, and British liaison officers with the French staffs in Paris. Top-level political relations between the two governments were carried on as usual through their ambassadors. The British Expeditionary Force (BEF) in France was under the overall command of French General Gamelin. The British commander of the BEF, General Gort, had a permanent liaison officer stationed in Gamelin's headquarters, and others in the headquarters of neighboring French armies.

The only change in this relationship came after the German invasion of the West, which began on May 10, 1940. Churchill, the newly appointed British Prime Minister, could see that communications between the two governments were too slow and cumbersome to permit them to deal effectively with the desperate situation created by the initial German victories. He therefore sent a personal representative to stay in constant touch with French Premier Reynaud. This representative was Major General Sir **Edward L. Spears**, a member of Parliament, who spoke perfect French, and who was a close personal friend of Churchill's. Spears was able to improve the exchange of communications between the two prime ministers, but by this time France was on the verge of collapse. Neither the French government nor the French armed forces were able to operate effectively by themselves, and real Allied coordination had become impossible. (Spears wrote a two-volume book about his experiences, *Assignment to Catastrophe*, which, after Churchill's great works, is perhaps the best personal-experience account of World War II.)

For the next year Britain was practically alone against Germany and Italy, so there were no allies to be coordinated. After Soviet Russia was attacked by Germany, Churchill welcomed the Russians as allies, even though he made clear that he still detested communism. There was little that could be done to coordinate the military efforts of these two allies, however, separated as they were by Nazi-dominated Europe. Furthermore, the British soon discovered that the suspicious Russians did not want any closer relationship between their two governments than was possible through their ambassadors.

Meanwhile, there had been some informal discussions between representatives of the British and American military staffs, to coordinate plans in case the United States should enter the war on the side of the British. In August, 1941, President Roosevelt and Prime Minister Churchill met at sea, off Argentia Bay, Newfoundland. At this so-called Atlantic Conference, the two leaders issued their famous Atlantic Charter, which denounced totalitarian aggression and proclaimed support to free peoples everywhere in the world. Though this was not an alliance, it was the beginning of a remarkable and close personal relationship between the leaders of the two great English-speaking nations. Since they had both been accompanied by leading military advisers, and since they discussed the possibilities of a war alliance, this may be considered as the beginning of the Allied organization for strategic direction of the war.

In Britain, of course, Mr. Churchill was primarily responsible for directing his nation's war effort, and he made this responsibility sharper by acting as Minister of Defence as well as Prime Minister.

2

He was assisted in developing overall policy by a War Cabinet, consisting of the principal civilian officials of the British Government. He was also assisted by the Chiefs of Staff Committee, which consisted of the military officers heading each of the three British armed services, who met with the War Cabinet, and were Mr. Churchill's principal military advisers. As a committee they were charged with issuing overall strategic orders for all British military operations.

Until the time of the attack on Pearl Harbor the United States did not have any kind of top-level civilian or military organization like that of the British. There were vague arrangements for coordinating the Army and the Navy, but these did not work very well. This lack of interservice coordination was partly responsible for American unreadiness for the Pearl Harbor attack.

It was immediately obvious to President Roosevelt that something should be done to remedy this situation. He recognized also that he would not be able to discuss war strategy with Churchill in an intelligent manner unless he had the same kind of organized military advice which the British Prime Minister received from his Chiefs of Staff Committee. But there were two problems which Roosevelt had to overcome before he could establish arrangements to obtain such advice.

The first problem was that the United States, unlike Britain, did not have an independent air force. The responsibility for military air operations was shared between the Army's Air Corps and the Navy's air arm. For this reason there was no single senior American officer who was in a position comparable to the Chief of the Air Staff of the Royal Air Force.

The second problem was the intense jealousy which existed between the U.S. Army and the U.S. Navy. This was partly due to their rival air organizations, but the jealousy extended further. Thus the Navy protested vigorously when Mr. Roosevelt initially appointed the Chief of the Army Air Corps as the air member of his military advisory committee. The Navy pointed out that this gave the Army two votes on the committee against one vote for the Navy.

Mr. Roosevelt solved these problems with an ingenious compromise. When the American Joint Chiefs of Staff Committee became regularly established, early in 1942, there were four members: General George C. Marshall, Chief of Staff of the Army; Admiral Ernest J. King, Chief of Naval Operations; General Henry H. Arnold, Chief of the Army Air Corps; and, to give the Navy two votes against the Army's two, Admiral William D. Leahy, a recently retired Navy officer, who was brought back to active duty with the title of "Chief of Staff for the President."

The first war meeting of the heads of the two governments and their military advisers took place in December, 1941, when Mr. Churchill came to Washington. The purpose of this conference was to reach agreement on Allied policy and strategy, and also to set up an Allied organization to supervise the agreed strategy.

From this meeting emerged the Combined Chiefs of Staff Committee, or CCS as it was usually called. This consisted of the British Chiefs of Staff Committee and the American Joint Chiefs of Staff. Since the British already had well-established and efficient procedures for the operation of their Chiefs of Staff Committee, the Combined Chiefs of Staff in general adopted British procedures. These same procedures, with some modification, were also adopted by the newly organized American Joint Chiefs of Staff Committee (or JCS, as it was usually known).

Since six of the seven members of the Combined Chiefs of Staff Committee were also responsible for commanding their own services in their headquarters in London and Washington, full meetings of the entire CCS Committee took place only when special conferences were arranged. There were ten of these conferences in all, during the war, and they are described in a later chapter of this book.

The British members of the CCS, however, pointed out to their

4

The Combined Chiefs of Staff confer in Cairo, Egypt, 1943.
U.S. Army Photograph

American partners that continuous strategic planning would be necessary, no matter how frequently full-scale conferences should be held. They also recognized the danger of possible lapses in Allied military coordination during the periods between conferences; this had happened between them and the French in 1940. The CCS was therefore kept in continuous session in Washington, and the British sent a senior military representative from each of their Services to represent them in the CCS headquarters in Washington.

Throughout the war President Roosevelt and Prime Minister Churchill kept in constant touch with each other through radio messages, but in order to make sure of complete and full understanding, they also met with each other several times, in different parts of the world. They were accompanied at these meetings by their senior military advisers, and so it was that the full-scale conferences of the CCS usually took place at the same time as the meetings between President and Prime Minister.

While the British and American members of the CCS were all concerned with all aspects of the war, the CCS itself gave immediate and close supervision only to the operations against Germany — in Europe, North Africa, and the western Mediterranean. Elsewhere the British and Americans divided between them the responsibility for direct control of military operations. The JCS was responsible for operations in the Pacific and the Southwest Pacific Theaters, and also for coordination with China; the British Chiefs of Staff controlled operations in the Middle East and Southeast Asia. Each nation also conducted its own military coordination with Russia, but this coordination was never very successful, and really became important only as the armies of Russia and the Western Allies approached each other in Germany toward the end of the war.

Strategic Leadership in the United States

FIVE MEN played a key role in the strategic leadership of the United States during World War II: President **Franklin Delano Roosevelt** and the four military members of the Joint Chiefs of Staff. During the four final months of the war, President **Harry S. Truman** replaced President Roosevelt, who died on April 12, 1945.

Important administrative roles in the conduct of the war were played by the civilian Secretaries — **Henry L. Stimson**, Secretary of War, and **Frank Knox** and **James V. Forrestal**, who were successively Secretaries of the Navy — and their able Assistant Secretaries. Their roles were so limited by the personal relationship of the President with the Joint Chiefs of Staff, however, that they are not considered in this book. Neither are the Secretaries of State — **Cordell Hull** and **Edward R. Stettinius** — since dynamic Mr. Roosevelt acted as his own Secretary of State during most of the war.

President Franklin D. Roosevelt signs the United States declaration of war with the Japanese Empire, December 8, 1941.
U.S. Army Photograph

Roosevelt's greatest weakness as a war leader was his failure to assure a proper balance between his military and his civilian subordinates in the formulation of strategy and of war policy. He never abandoned civilian supremacy over the military; his position of authority and responsibility was clear and undoubted from the beginning of the war until his death. Nevertheless, by his failure to make proper use of the Department of State, and his tendency to place principal reliance upon his military advisers, Roosevelt did reduce the proper and traditional role of civilian responsibility in the United States. It is a tribute to the stability of American civil-military relationships, and to the wisdom of his military advisers, that they were acutely aware of the great power and authority which they exercised, and were most cautious not to take improper advantage of it.

On the credit side, Mr. Roosevelt must be acknowledged as a wise and brilliant war leader in most respects. In the years immediately preceding the war, despite the opposition of a divided and penny-pinching Congress and the opposition of a loud isolationist minority of the people, he did everything within his power to prepare for the war which he foresaw. He did, however, make two serious mistakes during the war, both of which had far-reaching consequences.

The first was his adoption of the "unconditional surrender" slogan as a major Allied policy in the war. This lengthened World War II in Europe by several months. It offered no hope of a reasonably negotiated peace, and so it united Nazis and other Germans in a hopeless and costly struggle until the nation collapsed. In the case of Japan, fortunately, leaders on both sides recognized by August of 1945 that unconditional surrender was neither necessary nor desirable.

President Roosevelt's other great mistake was in his personal policies regarding Russia, and in his dealings with Generalissimo Stalin. Roosevelt was not "soft on communism," but, like many other Americans, he found it difficult to admire Russian resistance against Nazi aggression without at the same time trying to pretend that Stalin's evil dictatorship was a "democratic" ally. Furthermore, Roosevelt believed that he could influence Stalin. As a result, the United States gave to Russia the same kind of selfless material and military assistance that it gave so naturally to its appreciative British cousins. The Russians were never satisfied with what the Americans gave them, and thought the United States was weak in providing help without demanding political benefits in return.

President Truman exercised leadership as a war President during World War II for exactly four months. He inherited a system from President Roosevelt which he made no effort to change before the end of the war. In this he was wise. The war was virtually won by the time he came to the Presidency; all of the principal strategic decisions had been made, reconversion to peace had already begun.

President Truman was faced with one fateful decision during these closing days of the war: whether or not the atomic bomb was to be used against Japan. In deciding to use the bomb — a decision frequently criticized afterward — Mr. Truman did the only thing possible at the time and under the circumstances.

Fleet Admiral **William D. Leahy** had retired in 1939, after two years as Chief of Naval Operations, climaxing a distinguished naval career. In the immediate following years he served as Governor of Puerto Rico, and then as Ambassador to Vichy France.

As we have seen, when the Joint Chiefs of Staff was being established early in 1942, the Navy was worried that the Chief of Staff of the Army and the Chief of Staff of the Army Air Force would be able to outvote the Chief of Naval Operations. By appointing Admiral Leahy as his personal Chief of Staff, President Roosevelt assured two Navy votes against two Army votes within the Joint Chiefs of Staff. Admiral Leahy exercised his responsibilities seriously, deliberately, and wisely until his retirement in 1946. He made certain that the Joint Chiefs of Staff considered only matters that were "purely military." In the key strategical decision in the summer of 1944 — whether to return to the Philippines, as the Army wished, or to attack Formosa, as urged by the Navy — Leahy voted for the Army's position, and persuaded the Navy-minded President to do the same. Crusty, cantankerous Leahy was both competent and objective. He met his responsibilities well.

The most influential member of the Joint Chiefs of Staff was Army Chief of Staff **George C. Marshall.** He must share some of the blame, however, for the Army's lack of preparation for the Japanese attack on Pearl Harbor. But President Roosevelt did not hold this against

General George C. Marshall speaking to an audience of congressmen and military heads at the eighth annual National Council Dinner of the Reserve Officers Association of the United States, January 9, 1942.

U.S. Army Photograph

him, and kept Marshall on the job as Chief of Staff of the Army during all of World War II.

Marshall was a man of great intellectual ability who deserves major credit for the amazing expansion of the United States Army from a force of less than 200,000 men when he became Chief of Staff in 1939 to more than 8,000,000 men by early 1944. The administrative accomplishment of such a tremendous increase in size was in itself a tribute to Marshall and the organization which he headed as Chief of Staff. Particularly praiseworthy, however, is the fact that this enormously expanded military force remained competent, and was one of the most efficient military machines in the history of the world by the close of World War II.

Marshall probably saw the war in its global aspects more clearly than the President or any of his three colleagues on the Joint Chiefs of Staff. Although he and Admiral King frequently disagreed, the fact that they worked harmoniously together as a team is a tribute to Marshall's ability to compromise without weakness, and to negotiate major issues between the Services without rancor.

Cold, austere Marshall was neither a loved nor a lovable figure. He gained and earned respect as a genius of administration and organization, as well as a competent strategist.

Fleet Admiral **Ernest J. King** was a sailor's sailor. At the time of Pearl Harbor he was Commander in Chief of the U.S. Atlantic Fleet. Immediately after the disaster, he was appointed as Commander in Chief of the U.S. Fleet, to replace Admiral **H. E. Kimmel,** and early in 1942 he was assigned the additional duty of Chief of Naval Operations and the Navy member of the Joint Chiefs of Staff.

King was probably the best all-around military man on the Joint Chiefs of Staff in terms of operational, administrative, and strategic ability. Because of his responsibilities as Chief of Naval Operations, and a member of the Joint Chiefs of Staff, however, he, like Marshall, did not have a chance to demonstrate his leadership capability in battle. King probably lacked the breadth of strategic vision possessed by Marshall. Ever a fierce competitor, he was always concerned with the Navy's interest. His success is shown by the fact that no navy in history has ever so dominated the world's oceans as did the U.S. Navy at the zenith of King's career, August of 1945.

General of the Army **Henry H. Arnold** was Chief of the United States Army Air Corps when the war broke out. Because of this he became the air member of the Joint Chiefs of Staff. Junior in rank and age to the other three members of the Joint Chiefs of Staff, and at the same time a subordinate of General Marshall, Arnold was the least influential member of that group.

General of the Army Henry H. Arnold.

Nevertheless, as Commander of the Army Air Forces, Arnold performed well. He presided over an air establishment which grew from 22,000 officers and men and 3,900 planes to 2,500,000 officers and men and more than 200,00 aircraft.

Arnold, like many other airmen, was convinced that long-range strategic air bombardment would eventually prove to be the decisive factor in war. He played a great part in the development, deployment, and support of the great air armadas which went far (although not all the way) to prove his thesis in their destructive attacks on the industrial bases of Germany and Japan.

British Strategic Leadership

THE TOWERING FIGURE of World War II was **Winston Churchill,** one of the greatest men of all time. No civilian war leader has better understood the proper relationship of civilian authority to military leadership in war, or has had a clearer grasp of the essentials of strategy in its very broadest sense. His was the greatest single contribution to Allied victory in World War II.

Churchill's life was colorful, adventurous, and romantic. In 1898, as a young cavalry subaltern, after having observed an insurrection in Cuba and having already served in two active campaigns in India, he took part in the last great horse cavalry charge of the British army at the Battle of Omdurman, in the Sudan. Resigning from the army shortly thereafter, he was a war correspondent in the Boer War, was captured, but escaped. In the following years he entered active politics in England, while at the same time winning renown as a biographer and historian.

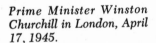

Prime Minister Winston Churchill in London, April 17, 1945.

As First Lord of the Admiralty (1911–16) he was responsible for the immediate readiness of the Royal Navy at the outset of World War I. He conceived the strategy of linking up with Russia by a thrust through the Dardanelles which would knock Turkey out of the war. The strategy was brilliant and sound, but was botched by an amazing number of errors and miscalculations by others who lacked Churchill's vision, energy, and thoroughness. Meanwhile, when other political and military leaders of lesser vision refused to adopt the concept of the tank as a weapon to break through the land stalemate in France, Churchill supported the development of tanks by the Admiralty. After the failure of the Dardanelles operations, he left politics and returned to the army. As a lieutenant colonel he commanded a battalion of the Royal Scots Fusiliers in what he termed "the squalid slaughter" of the trenches in France. Later he was recalled to the Government by Prime Minister Lloyd George to take over the vital post of Minister of Munitions, and at the end of the war was Minister of War and Air.

In the years between the World Wars Churchill, though usually a member of Parliament, was rarely included in the governments because of his outspoken criticism of all British attempts to appease the Fascist and Communist dictatorships. He continued to write, producing some of the finest histories and biographies written in the English language, while at the same time warning of the dangers posed to Britain and to the free world by the rapid rearmament of Germany, and by the ruthless aggressions of Italy and Japan. His advice was ignored until just before the outbreak of World War II, when Britain suddenly awoke to the deadly danger, and began to rearm.

When the war broke out, Prime Minister **Neville Chamberlain** appointed Churchill as First Lord of the Admiralty; there were cheers throughout the Royal Navy as the message flashed across the oceans: "Winston is back!" Forgetting his earlier criticisms of the Govern-

14

ment, Churchill made every effort to help Chamberlain rebuild Britain's decayed military strength; he was partly successful, but the German invasion of Western Europe in 1940 toppled Chamberlain's government as it smashed the Allied armies.

There was no longer doubt in Britain; with unanimous popular approval, the King appointed Churchill Prime Minister. Churchill embodied the resolute spirit of the British people as they stood alone and defiant against the Fascist masters of Europe. Amazingly, he inspired and directed a strategy which struck back with vigor, determination, and success against the Axis along the coast of France, throughout the Mediterranean, and across northern and eastern Africa. He joined with President Roosevelt to form "the Grand Alliance" which was to win eventual success in the war.

Acting not only as Prime Minister, but also as Minister of Defence, Churchill kept close and perceptive supervision and control over the actual conduct of the war. His was the vision which inspired many of the most brilliant strategic strokes and practical innovations of the war. His military subordinates were exasperated by Churchill's constant flow of ideas, suggestions, directions, and orders. Occasionally they balked, insisting that some of his imaginative ideas were impractical. In such cases Churchill always demanded proof, but never did he overrule any recommendation or decision of his Chiefs of Staff Committee. He never had any personal doubts as to the soundness of his own ideas, but he realized that the capable chiefs of the three military services were practical professionals more qualified than he to evaluate the details of tactical military operations.

On July 26, 1945, the war against Germany having been won, and that against Japan obviously approaching a successful conclusion, the British people, in a general election, decided to oust the Conservative Government and to try the Labor Party. Churchill had no choice but to bow to the popular will. Surprisingly, however, he regained power after the elections of 1951, and was Prime Minister

15

again until failing health forced his resignation in 1955.

Churchill not only did more than any man to *make* history in World War II, he also later did more than any man to *write* that same history; his six-volume work, *The Second World War*, is not only the finest personal memoir to come from the war, it is also the most important single reference work for all other historians of the war.

The professional military direction of the British war effort, under Churchill's overall supervision, was conducted by the Chiefs of Staff Committee, comprising the senior officer of each of the three military services: Chief of the Imperial General Staff for the Army, First Sea Lord for the Navy, and Chief of the Air Staff for the Air Force. When Churchill took over as Prime Minister on May 10, 1940, these posts were filled by General Sir **Edmund Ironside,** Air Marshal **Cyril L. Newall,** and Admiral Sir **Dudley Pound.**

On May 25, as the magnitude of the Allied defeat in the Battle of Flanders became evident, General Ironside, an old and close friend of Churchill, resigned, so that his post could be taken by a younger and more vigorous man. Churchill reluctantly accepted the resignation on May 27 and appointed General Sir **John Dill** as Chief of the Imperial General Staff. But Dill and Churchill found they could not work well together. In November, 1941, Dill was relieved, while his close friend, General Sir Alan Brooke, was appointed Chief of the Imperial General Staff.

In December, 1941, shortly after America's entry into the war, Churchill decided to appoint Dill as his personal representative in Washington, and also to represent the British Chiefs of Staff Committee in the Combined Chiefs of Staff headquarters in Washington. There could have been no better choice. Dill got along well with the Americans, and was one of the few men of any nationality with whom General Marshall had a really warm friendship.

Meanwhile, in September, 1940, the term of Air Chief Marshal

Sir John Dill.
Office of War Information

Newall expired, and Churchill decided that he should be replaced
by Air Chief Marshal **Charles F. A. Portal.** Thus, during the most
critical period of the war the Chiefs of Staff Committee consisted of
General Brooke, Admiral Pound, and Air Chief Marshal Portal. The
one final change in the composition of the Committee came in October, 1943, when a stroke forced Admiral Pound to resign; he died
a few days later. Admiral **Sir Andrew Cunningham** was appointed
the new First Sea Lord, and remained a member of the Committee
until the end of the war.

Sir Charles F. A. Portal.
Office of Chief of
Naval Operations

The strongest man of the Chiefs of Staff Committee, and the one most respected and relied upon by Churchill, was General Sir **Alan Brooke.** He had commanded the British II Corps in the disastrous campaign in Flanders, where he had performed brilliantly in the face of disaster. He had then commanded the new expeditionary force which Churchill sent to France, but which was withdrawn when France surrendered. Subsequently, as Commander in Chief of the Home Forces, he had greatly impressed Churchill with his planning and organizing ability.

As Chief of the Imperial General Staff, Brooke was one of the few men in the Government who had the courage as well as the intellectual ability to disagree with Churchill and to speak his opinion boldly. He recognized Churchill's brilliance, but soon discovered that the

Prime Minister did not understand, and was not interested in, the petty details of military administration. When he could, Brooke did his best to carry out all of Churchill's directives; but there were a number of occasions when he led the other members of the Chiefs of Staff Committee in respectfully but firmly opposing the Prime Minister's wishes or orders. Though both of the other members were senior in rank to the new Chief of the Imperial General Staff, both loyally acquiesced when Churchill appointed Brooke to the chairmanship of the Committee in March, 1942.

Brooke's incisive intellect, strong will, and abrupt manner brought him into frequent conflict with his American opposite numbers — and particularly with Admiral King, whose interest in the European war was secondary, just as Brooke's concern with the Pacific War was peripheral. It was a combination of these personality clashes, as well as the dynamics of realistic power politics, which kept Brooke from ever realizing his greatest ambition: to be commander of the Allied invasion of Europe.

Because of the overwhelming preponderance of American military and industrial strength, the Joint Chiefs of Staff insisted that the Supreme Commander for the Normandy invasion should be an American. Their objections to Brooke reinforced this American determination. Reluctantly Churchill accepted the facts of the relative power of the two nations. In turn, however, he refused to accept General Marshall as the invasion commander, and so Eisenhower was selected as a mutually agreeable and happy compromise.

Brooke was an administrator fully the equal of Marshall. His splendid performance in subordinate positions in combat, as well as his strategic competence displayed in the Chiefs of Staff Committee, would indicate that on balance he was Britain's first soldier in the war, in fact as well as in position and title. It would be difficult not to rate him as one of the very top generals of the war, with MacArthur, Manstein, and Rommel.

The oldest and senior member of the Chiefs of Staff Committee, Admiral of the Fleet Sir **Dudley Pound**, represented the very finest in British naval tradition. As a young captain in World War I, Pound commanded a battleship at Jutland. In the years between the wars his service was almost equally divided between the Admiralty and sea duty. He became First Sea Lord a few months before the outbreak of the war.

Since the Admiralty was the operational center for the Royal Navy, Pound was an operational commander as well as a member of the Committee supervising operations. (This was not true of the chiefs of the army or air staffs.) Despite this heavy double load, Pound performed his duties with tremendous ability and imperturbable self-confidence. Even after his first stroke — which he kept secret from Churchill, continuing to do his work, even though half-paralyzed — he refused to reduce the tempo of his activities. He soon realized, however, that he was physically unable to carry the load, and so he immediately resigned. He died a few days later, October 21, 1943.

Sir **Charles F. Portal** had distinguished himself as a fighter pilot in World War I. After a brief period as Commander in Chief of the RAF's Bomber Command, in 1940, he was selected by Churchill to be Chief of the Air Staff because he was, in Churchill's words, "the accepted star of the Air Force."

It was a wise choice. Portal had a unique ability to get along with people without any hypocrisy and without abandoning his own firm principles and beliefs. Like Brooke, he did not hesitate to speak unpleasant truths to the Prime Minister, even if this meant incurring the violence of Churchillian wrath. Portal and Brooke sometimes found themselves in disagreement on strategy and on policy; these professional arguments were eventually settled with good will, but only after long, earnest, and sometimes stormy debate. Yet the close personal friendship of these two strong and able men was never affected by their professional differences.

Portal established very cordial relations with the members of the American Joint Chiefs of Staff, who admired and respected his professional competence while trusting his evident sincerity and forthrightness. Brooke, recognizing his own inability to get along with the Americans, relied upon Portal as well as upon Sir John Dill to carry the brunt of the negotiating burden in many of the strategic debates between the British and the Americans.

Despite inevitable differences of national policy and of strategic aims between the United States and Britain, the military alliance which was directed by the Combined Chiefs of Staff was the most successful in history. Marshal of the Royal Air Force Portal played a most significant role in assuring that success.

Another man who contributed to the success of the Combined Chiefs of Staff and to the British war effort was Lieutenant General Sir **Hastings Ismay,** who was the chief of the military secretariat of the War Cabinet, and also acted as Churchill's personal Chief of Staff. Lord Ismay (known to his friends as "Pug") attended all meetings of the War Cabinet, and also sat in on all meetings of the Chiefs of Staff Committee as the Prime Minister's representative. To Ismay's good judgment, his military skill, and his deft diplomacy must go much credit for the relatively little friction which was found among the members of the Chiefs of Staff Committee, and between them and the Prime Minister. Ismay was trusted implicitly by Churchill, and he was admired, respected, and trusted by the three senior members of the Committee.

Although the British Chiefs of Staff Committee operated somewhat less formally than did the American Joint Chiefs of Staff, it was probably more efficient. If so, "Pug" Ismay was primarily responsible.

21

Strategic Leadership Among the Other Allies

Russia

IN THE Soviet Union, as in other dictatorships — friendly or unfriendly — during the war, the dictator combined in his own person the ultimate civilian and military leadership. In Russia, of course, the dictator was Generalissimo **Joseph Stalin,** who chose to use a military title during the war in order to emphasize his authority over all other Soviet military commanders.

Stalin, despite his humble beginnings, was a dictatorial autocrat in the tradition of the Russian czars. He was as ruthless as any of his predecessors in one thousand years of Russian history. He was as tyrannical as Hitler, but unlike the German dictator he was essentially level-headed and wise — as well as cynical and bloodthirsty — in the exercise of his dictatorship.

Although he exercised absolute authority over his military commanders as well as over the civilian government of the U.S.S.R., Stalin apparently did not inject himself into the details of military command. He made certain that all military strategy was consistent with his own political judgment of Russia's policy interests. Sometimes his judgment in such matters was good; sometimes it was bad.

Stalin's first political decision influencing military strategy was to attempt to hold Russia's frontiers against a German invasion. This was a very bad decision, and almost disastrous; it would have lost the war for Russia if Hitler had not made two worse decisions soon afterward. Stalin's decisions to hold at Moscow in 1941, and at Stalingrad in 1942, were both risky, but both succeeded. His decision not to help the Polish Resistance in Warsaw in the summer of 1944 was contemptible, but it assured Communist control of Poland after the war — which was what he wanted.

*Admiral of the Fleet Sir
Andrew Cunningham.*
Imperial War Museum

On balance, Stalin was a good and wise war leader of Russia; but he could not be trusted by his allies; he honored his promises only when it was useful to his power and to the expansion of international communism.

At the outset of World War II the Russian high command was still recovering from the disastrous effects of Stalin's ruthless purge of his leading military officers, which had taken place in 1937 and 1938. When that purge was over, more than half of the senior military professionals in the army had been executed. Since those who had been purged included the most aggressive, most imaginative leaders of the army, few of the remaining commanders had any inclination, even when they had the ability, to demonstrate any individuality or brilliance.

Stalin's two principal military advisers, however, were men of some

23

ability. The Chief of the General Staff was Marshal **Boris M. Sha-poshnikov,** an old Revolutionary soldier who had survived the purge by demonstrating his loyalty to Stalin. Though not a military genius, he combined considerable intelligence with many years of practical military and political experience. He was particularly fortunate in having as his deputy relatively young General **Georgi K. Zhukov,** Chief of the Army Staff, who was, as we have seen in an earlier volume, by far the most capable senior officer in the Russian army.

Stalin frequently ignored the advice of Shaposhnikov, but came to rely heavily on Zhukov. Late in 1942 Shaposhnikov retired from active duty due to poor health, and Zhukov went on to become — to Stalin's annoyance — the greatest Russian war hero. But, until the war was over, Zhukov remained the dictator's most trusted military adviser, even when he was exercising direct field command at the front.

France

As we have seen in an earlier volume, the top wartime leadership of France was weak and inefficient at the beginning of World War II. This was as true of the political leadership as it was of the military commanders. Premier **Paul Reynaud** was perhaps a cut above the mediocre average of French politicians of the times, but he proved to be weak and vacillating when disaster struck.

It is perhaps unfair to lump together all of the senior French generals and say that they were adequately represented by inept General Gamelin, whose failure we have noted in earlier volumes. But if they were worthy successors of the fighting French generals of World War I, none of them, apparently, had the chance to prove it.

Among the younger officers, however, France was eventually to find good leaders. A few of them, like **Charles de Gaulle,** showed their mettle by fighting vigorously even during the disastrous days of May and June, 1940. But, for most, the opportunity to display their capability did not come until after the Allied offensives began in

24

General Charles de Gaulle watching a victory parade in France, August 26, 1944.
U.S. Army Photograph

late 1942 and early 1943. That they had this opportunity was due to the continuing vigor and determination of de Gaulle who, by sheer willpower, had made himself the leader of the Free French movement soon after the collapse of France in June, 1940.

De Gaulle emerged from the war as the political leader of a revived French nation. He was disliked by both Churchill and Roosevelt, who found him most difficult to work with, but he earned their respect by the determination and skill with which he rebuilt the fighting power, the honor, and the glory of France. He was the only important leader in the war who had an opportunity to lead troops in battle as a soldier, and to direct his nation's policy as chief of state. He performed superbly in both roles. History will undoubtedly rank him as one of the greatest Frenchmen in history, and one of the greatest men of the twentieth century.

25

While de Gaulle was rallying Frenchmen to the Free French cause in London, the pitiful remnant of France, governed from Vichy, was under the nominal leadership of aged Marshal **Henri Philippe Pétain.** Pétain, the hero of Verdun in World War I, had been a staunch, if somewhat unimaginative, soldier who had risen to leadership of the French army in World War I under the overall guidance of Marshal Foch. Eighty-four years old when France was overwhelmed by Hitler's *blitzkrieg,* Pétain was under the influence of pro-Nazi French politicians. When called upon to succeed Reynaud and his collapsing government, Pétain had already decided to surrender, and ignored the pleas of Churchill and of patriots like de Gaulle to move the French government to North Africa, and to continue the war. After the surrender to Germany he remained the nominal ruler of Vichy France until the Germans occupied the entire country two and a half years later.

During most of that dismal period of French history, the real ruler of Vichy France was **Pierre Laval.** Prior to the outbreak of the war, Laval was one of the leading advocates of French appeasement of Hitler. After the French defeat Laval became a Nazi puppet and ruled France as a willing and eager instrument of Hitler. When Germany began to suffer reverses, Laval attempted to change his pro-Nazi policies, but he merely annoyed the Germans without convincing patriotic Frenchmen that he was anything other than an opportunist. He escaped from France after the liberation, but returned in 1945 to stand trial for treason. He conducted his defense ably, but was nevertheless convicted and executed.

The second most powerful man in the Vichy government was Admiral **Jean L. X. F. Darlan.** He had been commander in chief of the French navy at the outset of World War II, and performed competently. After the French surrender he was particularly embittered

Left to right — Admiral Darlan, General Eisenhower, Sir Andrew Cunningham, and General Giraud.

U.S. Army Photograph

by the British attack on the French fleet at Oran. His strongly anti-British attitude caused Hitler to approve his promotion to commander in chief of all Vichy-French forces early in 1942. Later that year he was also appointed French high commissioner in Africa, and was in Algiers when the Americans and British attacked in October, 1942. After two days of fighting he ordered all French forces in Africa to surrender to the Allies. In the following weeks he cooperated wholeheartedly with General Eisenhower to mobilize the resources of French Africa against the Axis. He was assassinated in Algiers on December 24, 1942.

Darlan was a patriotic and competent French naval officer who always attempted to do what he sincerely thought was in the best interests of his country. American and British public opinion linked him with the appeasers and collaborators led by Laval, but this was unjust.

China

The civilian and military head of the National Government of China was Generalissimo **Chiang Kai-shek.** As a young soldier, Chiang was a follower of Sun Yat-sen, the founder of the modern Chinese Republic. Through a combination of military and political skill Chiang Kai-shek became the military leader of the Republic of China and then, after reuniting most of the strife-torn country in the 1920's, became president. His rapid progress in uniting and strengthening China led to the Japanese invasion of China, which initiated World War II in Asia.

In subsequent years of defeat and despair, Chiang never lost hope in eventual victory over Japan. By a balance of force, favor, and diplomacy he held his country together during those terrible years, only to have it engulfed in a tragic and disastrous civil war just as victory against Japan was achieved. It is too early to assess Chiang's place in Chinese history; unquestionably he will be remembered as one of the most important leaders of China during the last two centuries.

Sharing a place in modern China's history with Chiang is his implacable enemy, **Mao Tse-tung,** who was the principal leader of the rebellious Chinese Communist Party in bitter civil war in the 1920's and 1930's. After the Japanese invasion, Mao and Chiang reached a temporary truce, but Mao used this cessation of hostilities with the National Government not so much to fight the common Japanese enemy as to establish a secure and powerful political and geographical base from which to launch all-out civil war again as soon as Japan surrendered. During much of the war the Chinese Communists and the Japanese had an unspoken and unsigned agreement whereby they left each other alone so as to concentrate their efforts against Chiang's National Government.

Generalissimo Chiang Kai-shek and Lieutenant General Joseph W. Stilwell.
U.S. Army Photograph

The Allied Conferences and Decisions

THERE WERE fourteen important Allied war conferences. Some of these were given special planning code names by the American and British CCS Committee. Sometimes they are referred to in history books and in memoirs by these code names, and sometimes simply

29

by the name of the place where the meeting took place. These meetings, and their code names, are listed below:

Conference Name	Place	Date
ATLANTIC	At sea (Argentia Bay, Newfoundland)	August 9–12, 1941
ARCADIA	Washington (1st)	December 24, 1941–January 14, 1942
BOLERO-LONDON	London	April 8–14, 1942
WASHINGTON	Washington (2nd)	June 18–21, 1942
CASABLANCA	Casablanca	January 14–23, 1943
TRIDENT	Washington (3rd)	May 12–25, 1943
QUADRANT	Quebec (1st)	August 14–24, 1943
MOSCOW	Moscow	October 19–30, 1943
SEXTANT	Cairo	November 22–26, and December 3–7, 1943
EUREKA	Teheran	November 28–30, 1943
OCTAGON	Quebec (2nd)	September 12–16, 1944
ARGONAUT-CRICKET	Malta	January 30–February 2, 1945
ARGONAUT-MAGNETO	Yalta	February 4–9, 1945
TERMINAL	Potsdam	July 16–August 2, 1945

The important aspects of these conferences are summarized briefly in the following paragraphs.

Atlantic Conference, *August 9-12, 1941*

Principal Participants

President Roosevelt, Prime Minister Churchill, and military staffs; Lord Beaverbrook, Harry Hopkins, Sumner Welles.

Decisions

No major strategic decisions were reached, save for confirmation of the American agreement to undertake responsibility for all Atlantic convoys west of Iceland. Lend-lease, and supply of munitions to Russia were discussed.

Other Results

The principal result of the meeting was the issuance of the Atlantic Charter which, for security reasons, was dated two days after the closing of the conference. The Atlantic Charter, with its eight principles for a better postwar world, was in fact the genesis of the United Nations. The name "United Nations" was first used in the published joint, or "United Nations," declaration of January 1, 1942, in which all of the Allied nations pledged themselves to support the principles of the Atlantic Charter. (Actually this declaration was prepared at the Arcadia Conference, which follows.)

Arcadia Conference, *December 24, 1941-January 14, 1942*

Principal Participants

President Roosevelt, Prime Minister Churchill, and military staffs.

Decisions

1. The principal Allied war effort was to be directed first against Germany; defeat of Japan and Italy would be subordinated to this main effort.

2. Prior to concentrating efforts against Germany, some basic undertakings would be necessary to prevent losing the war before it could be won; among these basic undertakings were: (a) to secure the main areas of war industry in the United States and Great Britain; (b) to maintain essential lines of communication in the Atlantic and Pacific; (c) in the Atlantic area, to occupy French North Africa; (d) in the Pacific area, to hold positions to safeguard "vital interests"

and, if possible, to deny Japan access to raw materials vital to her war effort.

3. To establish the Combined Chiefs of Staff Organization to direct the British-American war effort.

London Conference, *April 8-14, 1942*

Principal Participants

Prime Minister Churchill, Harry Hopkins, General Marshall, British Chiefs of Staff Committee.

Decisions

The British Government and Chiefs of Staff reluctantly accepted the American plan for "Bolero," a proposal for an immediate buildup of American forces in the United Kingdom in preparation for an invasion of Nazi Europe in 1943 ("Operation Roundup"), or possibly 1942 ("Operation Sledgehammer"). British reluctance was due to belief that the Allies would not be ready in time, and that other "basic undertakings" should come first. The Americans felt that the British were too concerned with holding on to their empire, rather than concentrating on the defeat of Germany.

Washington Conference, *June 18-21, 1942*

Principal Participants

President Roosevelt, Prime Minister Churchill, the Combined Chiefs of Staff.

Decisions

1. Abandonment of the idea of "Sledgehammer," a possible invasion of Europe in 1942; instead, agreement was reached on an invasion of French North Africa in November.

2. Reaffirmation of the concept of "Roundup" (invasion of Europe in 1943); increased buildup of U.S. air forces in the United Kingdom for this purpose.

President Franklin Delano Roosevelt with Prime Minister Churchill at Casablanca.
U.S. Air Force Photo

3. Agreements on pooling of British-American information and resources for atomic research in the U.S.

Casablanca Conference, *January 14-23, 1943*

Principal Participants

President Roosevelt, Prime Minister Churchill, Combined Chiefs of Staff.

Decisions

1. To continue the current assault against Germany with subsidiary aims of drawing enemy weight from Russia and knocking Italy out of the war.

2. Upon completion of the Tunisian campaign to invade Sicily ("Operation Husky") in June or July.

3. To give high priority to a combined bomber offensive against Germany and German-occupied Europe from the United Kingdom.

4. To advance toward the Philippines through the Central and Southwest Pacific areas.

5. To build up U.S. air forces in the China-Burma-India region, with a view to a combined overland and amphibious offensive in Burma in the fall of 1943 ("Operation Anakim"), with such assistance from U.S. naval forces and landing craft from the Pacific as would be necessary.

6. To increase assistance to China.

7. To terminate hostilities only upon the "unconditional surrender" of the enemy.

Trident Conference, *May 12-25, 1943*

Principal Participants

President Roosevelt, Prime Minister Churchill, Combined Chiefs of Staff.

Decisions

1. Agreement on a cross-Channel invasion of Europe ("Operation Overlord"); to be initiated on target date of May 1, 1944.

2. "Operation Overlord" was to be preceded by an intensified air offensive from the United Kingdom.

3. Operations following the conquest of Sicily were to be designed to knock Italy out of the war.

4. Ploesti oil fields in Romania were to be bombed from Mediterranean bases.

5. An increase in material assistance to China, in particular for the buildup of Chennault's Fourteenth Air Force.

6. In the Pacific the Japanese were to be completely ejected from the Aleutians, with an intensification of operations against Japan, particularly by operations in the Central Pacific.

President Roosevelt and Prime Minister Churchill take time off to rest at Casa-Blanca Conference.

U.S. Army Photograph

7. Stilwell's request for increased American ground forces in Burma was disapproved; small-scale amphibious operations were to be undertaken along the Burmese coast.

Quadrant Conference, *August 14-24, 1943*

Principal Participants

President Roosevelt, Prime Minister Churchill, Secretary of State Hull, Foreign Minister Eden, Chinese Foreign Minister T. V. Soong, Combined Chiefs of Staff.

Decisions

1. The crushing of Germany remained the prime Allied objective; however, the war against Japan was to be prosecuted with the greatest intensity compatible with the demands of the concentration against Germany.

*General Henry H. Arnold
and Sir Dudley Pound at
the Quebec Conference.*
U.S. Army Photograph

2. The primary effort against Germany was to consist of the intensified Combined Bomber Offensive ("Operation Pointblank") to smash German military and economic strength, followed by "Operation Overlord" on the target date of May 1, 1944, in turn followed by a landing in southern France ("Operation Anvil," later "Operation Dragoon"). (Churchill strongly opposed the southern France landing, preferring operations in the Balkans or northern Adriatic area.)

3. Plans for the invasion of Italy were to be hastened due to the fall of Mussolini's government.

4. Increased efforts were to be made to draw the Soviet Union into full concert with the Western Allies.

5. De Gaulle's French Committee of National Liberation was recognized as the unquestioned representative of Free French people and forces opposing the Axis.

36

6. Advances against Japan were to be continued in the Central and Southwest Pacific Theaters.

7. The Southeast Asia Command (SEAC) was established with Admiral Lord Louis Mountbatten as Supreme Commander and General Stilwell as his deputy; outside SEAC Stilwell remained responsible to Generalissimo Chiang Kai-shek in China.

8. An offensive in North Burma was approved for February, 1944, to facilitate the supply of China by an overland route.

Moscow Conference, *October 19-30, 1943*

Principal Participants

Secretary of State Hull, Foreign Minister Eden, Foreign Minister Molotov. The Chinese Ambassador to Russia participated slightly.

Decisions

1. A "Four-Power Declaration" was issued; the Allies agreed to continue the war until the unconditional surrender of the Axis powers, and to cooperate in establishment of a world organization for peace after the war.

2. Plans were made to establish a three-power European Advisory Commission to study and make recommendations on problems relating to the termination of the war in Europe (occupation zones, boundary questions, and the like).

3. Plans were made to establish an Advisory Council on Italy to coordinate Allied policy on Italy, consistent with a determination to destroy fascism and to restore democratic self-government in Italy.

4. Allied determination to restore the independence of Austria was expressed.

5. A warning was issued that atrocities and war crimes committed by individual Germans would be punished.

Quebec Conference. Seated, left to right: Canadian Prime Minister Mackenzie King, President Franklin D. Roosevelt, and Prime Minister Winston Churchill; standing, left to right: General Henry H. Arnold, Air Chief Marshal Sir Charles F. Portal, General Sir Alan Brooke, Admiral E. J. King, Field Marshal Sir John Dill, General George C. Marshall, Sir Dudley Pound, Admiral W. D. Leahy.

Teheran Conference. Left of Prime Minister Churchill stands British Foreign Minister Anthony Eden. Left of Mr. Eden is Sir John Dill. Premier Stalin is flanked by General Klementi E. Voroshilov and Foreign Minister Vyacheslav M. Molotov.

U.S. Army Photograph

Sextant Conference, *November 22-26 and December 3-7, 1943*

Principal Participants

President Roosevelt, Prime Minister Churchill, Generalissimo Chiang Kai-shek, Combined Chiefs of Staff.

Decisions

1. Agreement was reached during the first session on an offensive in Burma ("Operation Champion"), to include an amphibious operation against the coast, and the participation of the Chinese Y-Force in Yünnan; North Burma was to be cleared in early 1944 to open a land route to China. At the second session of the conference the CCS decision to cancel the amphibious operation (reached at Teheran

after the first session of the Cairo Conference) left the plan unsettled, since Chiang refused to commit himself to a Y-Force offensive in the north without a simultaneous amphibious operation in the south.

2. Approval of a plan to base B-29 Superfortresses in China ("Operation Twilight").

3. A timetable for operations in the Central and Southwest Pacific areas was established.

4. A unified command was established in the Mediterranean, initially under General Eisenhower as Supreme Allied Commander.

5. Three-power agreement was reached, which provided, in essence: to continue the war against Japan relentlessly; to return former Chinese territories to China after the war; and "that in due course Korea shall become free and independent."

Eureka Conference, *November 28-30, 1943*

Principal Participants

President Roosevelt, Prime Minister Churchill, Generalissimo Stalin, Combined Chiefs of Staff, Russian military staff.

Decisions

1. In compliance with Russian requests, the Western Allies agreed to give operations "Overlord" and "Anvil" priority over all other operations. (It was diversion of landing craft to "Anvil" that forced cancellation of the previously planned amphibious operations against Burma.) Stalin agreed on a major Russian offensive in coordination with the "Overlord" invasion of northwestern Europe.

2. Russia agreed to commit Soviet forces against Japan after the defeat of Germany.

3. The three governments agreed to maintain the independent sovereignty and territorial integrity of Iran.

Octagon Conference, *September 12-16, 1944*

Principal Participants

President Roosevelt, Prime Minister Churchill, Combined Chiefs of Staff.

Decisions

1. The war against Japan was to be prosecuted with increasing intensity, as permitted by events in Europe.

2. Admiral Mountbatten was given the primary mission of recapturing Burma as soon as possible; "Operation Dracula" (amphibious assault to capture Rangoon) and an overland operation, aimed at a minimum to reopening of the land route to China, were to be undertaken by March 15, 1945.

3. Britain's share in operations in the Pacific Ocean areas was to be increased, particularly in the air and at sea, as forces could be released from the European region.

4. Operations against Japan would culminate with an Allied invasion of Kyushu, in October, 1945 ("Operation Olympic"); this was to be followed by an invasion of the Tokyo Plain on Honshu in December ("Operation Coronet").

Argonaut-Cricket Conference (Malta), *January 30, and February 2, 1945*

Principal Participants

President Roosevelt, Prime Minister Churchill, Combined Chiefs of Staff.

Decisions

This was essentially a preparatory conference between the British and American delegations to the Magneto (Yalta) Conference. No major decisions were reached.

41

Argonaut-Magneto Conference (Yalta), *February 4-9, 1945*

Principal Participants

President Roosevelt, Prime Minister Churchill, Generalissimo Stalin, Combined Chiefs of Staff, Russian military staff.

Decisions

1. General military agreements were reached regarding coordination of final military operations in Germany, and the terms of surrender which would be offered to Germany.

2. Agreement was reached on Allied zones of occupation in Germany.

3. Russian claims to portions of prewar Poland were accepted; in turn Poland was to be compensated by territory to be taken from Germany.

4. Russia reaffirmed its intention to enter the war against Japan within three months of the end of the war in Europe; in return the Western Allies agreed to provide substantial amounts of equipment and to urge China to grant Russia certain rights in Manchuria.

5. The principles of the Atlantic Charter were reaffirmed.

Terminal Conference, *July 16, and August 2, 1945*

Principal Participants

President Truman, Prime Minister Churchill (initially), Prime Minister Attlee (subsequently), Generalissimo Stalin, Combined Chiefs of Staff, Russian military staff.

Decisions

1. Issuance on July 26 of the Potsdam Declaration by the Western Allies (with China agreeing; Russia abstained since she was still at peace with Japan) calling for Japan to surrender unconditionally without delay, or else face "utter destruction"; the declaration implied that if Japan surrendered, her territorial integrity and traditional

Potsdam Conference. The Big Three are shown shaking hands outside the palace. Left to right: Prime Minister Winston Churchill, President Harry S. Truman, and Generalissimo Josef Stalin.

institutions would be respected but her war-making capability would be destroyed.

2. Agreements on British participation in the final land, sea, and air operations against Japan.

3. Russia reaffirmed her intention to enter the war against Japan in August.

4. It was agreed to establish a Council of Foreign Ministers to meet periodically to draft peace treaties and to handle the numerous difficult political questions on postwar Europe, a number of which had remained outstanding due to lack of agreement at the conference.

5. Preliminary agreements on reparations were made, giving to Russia much that she demanded from Germany and Axis satellites of eastern Europe.

6. Agreement was reached on the trial of Axis war criminals.

43

Axis Strategic Leadership

Hitler as a War Leader

MORE THAN any single person, Adolf Hitler, the evil dictator of Germany, was responsible for World War II, and for the terrible death, destruction, and tragedy caused by the war. At his orders, more than 5,000,000 Jews were killed and cruelly tortured by starvation, by shooting, and particularly in the horrible gas chambers and incinerators of concentration camps like Buchenwald and Belsen. Hitler was perfectly willing to sacrifice millions of men, women, and children, Germans as well as others, in order to increase his own power and to make Germany the greatest nation in the world.

In the process of trying to gain these objectives, Hitler proved himself a brilliant, cunning, and ruthless politician. He also demonstrated an unusually keen awareness of the basic elements of military strategy. This strategic brilliance for a while caused many people, including some of the top military men of Germany, to think that he was a military genius, and that under his leadership the German army was unbeatable.

After some of his early, spectacular successes, it became evident that Hitler's strategic capability was far from perfect and, even more significant, that he did not understand the relationship of military administration and tactics to strategy. By this time, however, he had become so convinced that he was a military genius that he blamed the results of his errors on other people, and took over increasing personal control of military affairs. Germany was already doomed to lose the war, but his mistakes, and his stubborn refusal to follow the advice of his trained military advisers, hastened that defeat.

Hitler's principal strategic mistakes were his failure to understand either the determination or the basic fighting capabilities of the British people; his failure to understand the nature of the overwhelm-

44

Ribbentrop, Kurusu, and Hitler during the Japanese Ambassador's last visit to Germany, February 3, 1941.

U.S. Army Photograph

ing industrial and war-making power of the United States; his foolish determination to make war against America, Britain, and Russia at the same time; his failure, after having gotten his nation engaged in such a war, to fully mobilize all German industrial power until 1943; and his shortsighted mistreatment of anti-Communist minorities in Russia, who were eager to help Germany overthrow Stalin's tyrannical dictatorship.

Hitler's most important individual military blunders were made in Russia, where he took over personal direction of the fighting. By diverting the most mobile German forces to surround the Russian defenders of Kiev and the Dnieper Bend, in 1941, he lost his opportunity to take Moscow in October or early November. In the summer of 1942 he committed two blunders at once in diverting great forces to his effort to take Stalingrad, while elsewhere needlessly inviting Russian counterattacks against the flanks of his troops streaming into the Caucasus. Finally, once the Russians had obtained the initiative in the war in the east, and (with American and British help) had mobilized an overwhelming superiority of forces, Hitler refused to let his commanders fight flexible, mobile warfare, as they wished, on a much reduced front. Hitler stubbornly insisted upon holding every bit of territory which his troops had captured. As a result the Germans lost millions of men unnecessarily in trying to carry out hopeless defenses, with the result that they did not have enough men to defend even their own frontiers when they were driven back to the borders of Germany.

The German General Staff

If Hitler was a military blunderer, his generals were not. We have already seen (in an earlier book) how the German General Staff contributed to the development of a military system which, for one hundred years, probably produced more outstanding combat soldiers than have ever emerged in one nation in any similar period of history. Strangely, however, there were two weaknesses in this system which prevented Germany from making the best possible uses of its military resources in World War II. The first weakness was the reluctance of the General Staff in particular, and the German officer corps in general, to overthrow Hitler when his evil nature and intentions became obvious. The second weakness was a basic organizational defect — lack of interservice coordination — which enabled Hitler to seize complete control over the General Staff during the war.

The Germans had no unified interservice staff such as existed in Britain at the outset of World War II, or as was created in the United States in late 1941 and early 1942. Nor did the Germans and their Axis partners make any attempt to establish an overall international strategic planning and control staff like the Anglo-American Combined Chiefs of Staff. Such coordination as existed between the Germans and Italians was simply due to the dominance of more efficient and more powerful German commanders and staffs when German and Italian forces served together, as in North Africa and Sicily. There was neither reason nor opportunity for the German and Japanese war leaders to coordinate their activities; it is doubtful if either would have been willing to trust the other to any great degree.

In Germany itself, Hitler exercised his personal control over the three independent and uncoordinated military services through a small personal staff. This was entitled the *Oberkommando der Wehrmacht* (Armed Forces Supreme Command), and was generally known as OKW. The individuals on this staff were picked for their loyalty to Hitler and to the Nazi Party, not for any special military capability. The OKW never operated as a unified General Staff for the coordination of the three services.

The famous German General Staff, which had been in existence for over one hundred years, was an organization which controlled only the army. In World War II it was called *Oberkommando des Heeres*, or Army Supreme Command, and was known as OKH. The navy and the air force each had a similar staff organization, but neither was as well known or as efficient as the OKH.

When the German armies invaded Russia, in mid-1941, the Army General Staff, or OKH, planned and controlled the operation, which demanded practically all of the attention of the staff. What little coordination was attempted of relatively small German forces engaged elsewhere — principally in North Africa and Yugoslavia — was exercised directly by Hitler, through the OKW.

After the German armies were repulsed before Moscow, Hitler dismissed General von Brauchitsch, Commander in Chief of the Army, and took personal command of operations in Russia himself. He kept General Franz Halder on as Chief of Staff, but from that time on OKH became merely a theater, or area staff, responsible only for control of operations in Russia and eastern Europe.

This meant that from that time on Hitler had two general staffs: the OKH for Russia, and the OKW for the other two fronts in western and southern Europe. As operations grew active in those two theaters in 1943 and 1944, Hitler built up OKW until it became almost as large as the OKH. By thus creating two general staffs, Hitler destroyed both the mission and the efficiency of the traditional German General Staff as a coordinating agency. This was partly because he mistrusted, hated, and feared the aristocratic army officers, and partly because he did not realize the dangers of uncoordinated military operations on different fronts.

German Staff Leaders

The most thankless job a German general could have was to act as chief of the OKH after Hitler assumed command in Russia in December, 1941. Two men held this position during most of the remaining three and a half years of the war. First was **Franz Halder,** who had been Chief of the General Staff under Brauchitsch since 1939, and who retained the post under Hitler until September, 1942. A meticulous, hardworking, conscientious, but uninspiring soldier, Halder never had Hitler's confidence. Though he often dared to stand up to the dictator, whom he hated intensely, he never had nerve enough to resign. He served Hitler as a very senior administrative clerk, but never as a true chief of staff.

Halder's more youthful successor, Colonel General **Kurt Zeitzler,** remained in the post for nearly two years, and was at first considerably more successful. Though lacking real authority, Zeitzler had a forceful personality and was able to influence the dictator on a number of occasions. Hitler, however, became increasingly annoyed by Zeitzler's stubbornness, and particularly by his support of field commanders like Manstein. Zeitzler submitted his resignation five times,

General Franz Halder.

Field Marshal Wilhelm Keitel
U.S. Army Photograph

and five times Hitler refused to accept it. The dictator suspected him of complicity in the assassination plot of July 20, 1944, and relieved him that day, putting Guderian in the spot "temporarily" for more than eight months.

Human nature being what it is, there were many "yes-men" among the German officer corps, who did everything that they could to make a good impression upon the dictator. The two most notorious of these were Field Marshal **Wilhelm Keitel,** and Colonel General **Alfred Jodl.** In 1938, to reduce the power of the Army General Staff,

Nazi Chief of Staff Colonel General Alfred Jodl at SHAEF headquarters at Rheims, France, waits to sign unconditional surrender terms, May 6, 1945.
U.S. Army Photograph

Hitler had created the OKW and appointed Keitel as chief of this special and personal staff. Keitel was an officer of mediocre abilities, who managed always to keep himself in Hitler's favor by shameless toadying. He was distrusted by all of the army's senior officers. Jodl, who was the chief of the OKW Operations Staff, was a much more intelligent man, with considerable military talent. Though almost as shameless as Keitel in currying favor with Hitler, he was able to give the dictator some useful military advice, and prevented him from making a number of blunders. Both Keitel and Jodl were convicted as war criminals at Nuremberg and were hanged.

Japanese Strategic Leadership

General **Hideki Tojo** was the principal political as well as military leader of Japan during the war. When he became Prime Minister of

General Hideki Tojo.
U.S. Office of
War Information

Japan, in October, 1941, he immediately began preparations for war. In the early months of the conflict Tojo did not intervene personally in the conduct of operations, leaving supervisory tasks to General **Hajime Sugiyama,** Chief of the Army General Staff, and Admiral of the Fleet **Osami Nagano,** Chief of the Naval General Staff.

In 1943, after a series of Japanese defeats in the Pacific, Tojo took over the positions of War Minister and of Chief of the Japanese Imperial Headquarters (the combined Army and Navy General Staffs), to exercise virtual dictatorship over the nation and its war effort. In July, 1944, however, American landings on the Mariana Islands caused the fall of Tojo's cabinet, and the end of his influence on the conduct of the war. After the Japanese surrender, Tojo was tried as a war criminal for the part he had played in causing the war. He was convicted and hanged.

51

Admiral Osami Nagano, shortly before his death from pneumonia at the 361st U.S. Army Station Hospital in Tokyo, January 5, 1947.

U.S. Army Photograph

As we have seen earlier, the nature of the war in the Pacific, due in part to the initial Japanese strategic plan, and in part to the effectiveness of American submarine and air operations, caused the Japanese to fight a number of widely separated, isolated, and uncoordinated campaigns and battles. There was not, therefore, very much opportunity for the Japanese Imperial Headquarters to act as an overall strategic coordinating agency. Only the Commander in Chief of the Combined Fleet was able to shift forces and to exercise true strategic leadership. As we have seen, this leadership was spotty, though Admirals **Isoroku Yamamoto** and **Soemu Toyoda** were both capable commanders and strategists.

Mussolini confers with Ribbentrop in Florence, Italy, October 28, 1940.

U.S. Army Photograph

Italian Strategic Leadership

Before the war the Italian dictator, **Benito Mussolini,** had visions of a new Roman Empire, with Italy dominating the Mediterranean, southern Europe, and North Africa. Mussolini, however, had neither the personal force and political-strategic skill of a Hitler, nor the support of a powerful and disciplined nation like Germany. He proved to be weak and vacillating; his people had no interest in the war; and his top military and naval commanders had little confidence either in themselves or their men.

When the Allies prepared to assault mainland Italy, the Italian people overthrew the Mussolini government. Propped up by the Germans, Mussolini continued the pretense of a government in the German-occupied areas of north Italy. When German resistance collapsed, he attempted to flee to Germany, only to be captured and brutally killed by Italian Resistance fighters.

The Italian command organization was no more distinguished than the political leadership of Mussolini, or than the almost uniformly disastrous combat leadership of the generals and admirals. The air force was perhaps a cut above the army and the navy in organizational and operational efficiency, but the difference was not great. During his relatively brief period as a wartime chief of staff, Field Marshal **Pietro Badoglio** showed himself to be an honorable officer who at least recognized some of his nation's military deficiencies. When he was unable to prevent Mussolini from exposing these deficiencies, he resigned. His less distinguished successors were little better than administrative clerks, responding as well as they could to the demands and directions of the efficient and contemptuous Germans.

The revitalization of the Italian armed forces, after Italy joined the Allies, was in part due to Badoglio's influence as prime minister, and in part to an almost miraculous resurgence of national honor as the Italians sought revenge against both Mussolini and the arrogant Germans.

The Cost of World War II*

Nations	Total Forces Mobilized	Military Dead	Military Wounded	Civilian Dead	Economic and Financial Costs
United States	14,900,000	292,100	571,822	Negligible	$350 billion
United Kingdom	6,200,000	397,762	475,000	65,000	150 "
France	6,000,000	210,671	400,000	108,000	100 "
Soviet Union	20,000,000	7,500,000	14,012,000	10-15,000,000	200 "
China	6-10,000,000	500,000	1,700,000	1,000,000	No estimate
Germany	12,500,000	2,850,000	7,250,000	500,000	300 billion
Italy	4,500,000	77,500	120,000	40-100,000	50 "
Japan	7,400,000	1,506,000	500,000	300,000	100 "
All Other Participants	20,000,000	1,500,000	No estimate	14-17,000,000†	350 "
Totals**	100,000,000	15,000,000	No estimate	30,000,000	$1,600 billion

Notes:

* Many of these figures (compiled from various sources) are approximations or estimates, since official figures are misleading, missing, or contradictory in many instances.

† This includes approximately 6,000,000 Jews of Germany and all occupied European nations, and approximately 4,500,000 Poles.

** In total deaths and in economic and financial costs World War II was about five times as expensive as World War I; in military deaths alone, it was almost twice as costly.

Index

The following is a brief description of the contents of Volumes 1-18:

61

Volume 18 — STRATEGIC DIRECTION